Petunia Twinkletoes
The Happy Valley Twins

Samantha Vega

Meadow House Press

For Bia. Thank you for asking me to write this story.
For Lila. Thank you for helping me make it better.
For Sylvia and Pearl. Thank you for the endless inspiration.

Contents

Copyrights	IV
Map of Happy Valley Farm	1
1. Chapter 1	2
2. Chapter 2	6
3. Chapter 3	9
4. Chapter 4	12
5. Chapter 5	16
6. Chapter 6	20
7. Chapter 7	23
8. Chapter 8	28
9. Chapter 9	31
10. Chapter 10	35
11. Chapter 11	39
Keep in touch!	42

Copyright © 2023 by Samantha Vega

All rights reserved.

No part of this publication may be reproduced, distributed, or transmitted in any form or by any means, including photocopying, recording, or other electronic or mechanical methods, without the prior written permission of the publisher, except as permitted by U.S. copyright law. For permission requests, contact meadowhousepress@gmail.com

The story, all names, characters, and incidents portrayed in this production are fictitious. No identification with actual persons (living or deceased), buildings, and products is intended or should be inferred. Happy Valley Farm is a fictitious place.

Book Cover and Illustrations by Winda Mulyasari

1st edition 2024

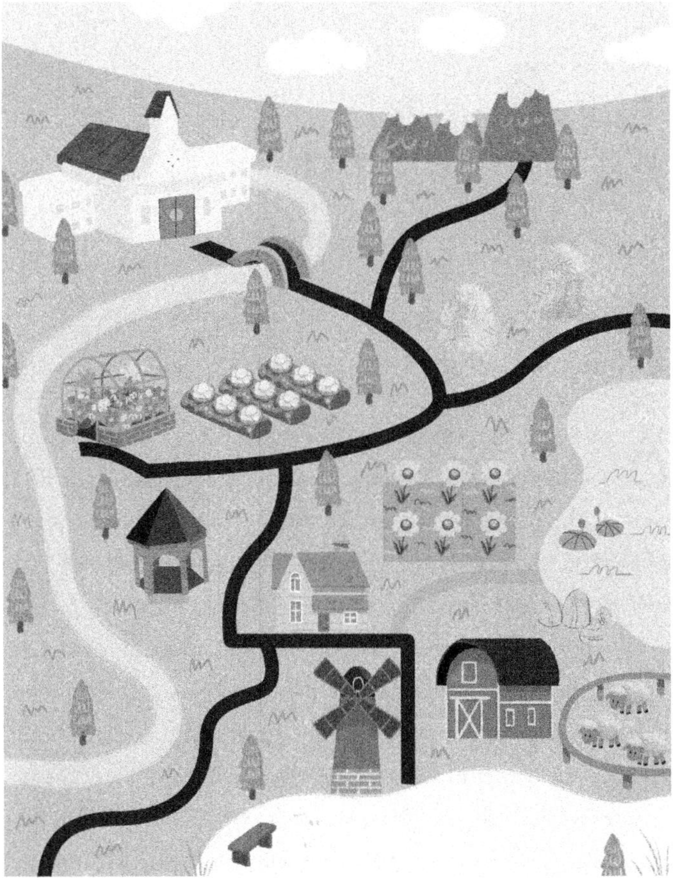

Chapter 1

A spring breeze sailed through Happy Valley Farm. Benjamin Costa put down his comic book and peered out of the little window in his snug new room. He could finally see the bright sun shining over the brick watchtower just beyond the grove of willow trees. He shouted to his twin sister, "Elisa! Let's go outside!"

The spring season was extra rainy, and the twins had been stuck inside for days. They hadn't gotten a chance to explore their new home since they moved to Happy Valley Farm from the city last week. Their mom was the new farm manager, and she told them all about the adventure that awaited them. There was a big red barn with farm animals and a shady picnic cove near the watchtower. The vegetable patch and flower garden bloomed next to a large greenhouse. A forested trail ended at a sandy river bank and a wooden walkway led to a small lake. And, of course, there was the old farmhouse by the orchard where they lived with their mom in the cozy apartment upstairs.

Benjamin leaped from the top bunk and ran to meet Elisa downstairs in the library. Old, colorful books lined the walls from floor to ceiling. Elisa and Benjamin liked to use the rolling bookcase ladder to pretend they were pirates when no one was around to scold them. Elisa sat at her perch on the soft cushion under the big bay windows. Glittering light of every color streamed in through the glass, making Elisa look like a rainbow fairy.

"Where should we go first?" Elisa asked. "Mom's helping out in the greenhouse, so we have all afternoon to explore."

"Let's climb to the top of the watchtower so we can see the view now that the clouds are gone," said Benjamin thoughtfully.

"Great idea!" Elisa replied.

The twins grabbed their backpacks and ran out the front door. They raced through the blooming flower garden towards the shady willow trees. The watchtower stood nearby, so tall it almost blocked the sun.

Elisa pointed to a bright glow in the diamond-shaped window at the top of the tower, but it wasn't the sun. "Benjamin, check out that cool light! Let's race to the top!"

Panting and exhausted, the twins finally made it to the top of the tower. The glow was even brighter from there.

"I bet it's a yellow sapphire!" Benjamin said excitedly.

A tiny hum coming from the glow made them gasp in surprise. The glow flickered and moved softly until it finally revealed itself.

Elisa gasped. "It's a fairy!"

Chapter 2

A small, bright figure barely larger than a kitten's paw buzzed in the rafters overhead. It *was* a fairy! She had long, flowing hair the color of the afternoon sun. Brightness bounced in every direction. Hints of cinnamon bread and apple blossoms wafted about.

A little hum and giggle emerged from the fairy. "Hum dee dum too la loo. What took you so long?! I've been waiting up here ever since the sun came out!"

Benjamin and Elisa stared at the fairy and then at each other.

"Hmmm? What do you say? The sun won't be out forever and we have work to do!" the little fairy said. Her hazel eyes shined with determination and delight.

Elisa asked, "What work?" just a beat after Benjamin questioned, "Who are you?"

"Silly dilly dew drop, what do you mean, who am I?" Sparkles of light flared out from her shadow in cheerful protest. "How could I be anyone other than Petunia Twinkletoes?"

The twins looked at each other with puzzled faces. They had never heard of a Petunia anything, much less a teensy glowing fairy!

"Well, Benjamin and Elisa. I know who YOU are. You're the helpers. Our Newsy Twosies."

They stared some more. Elisa's big brown eyes were wide as sunflowers, wider than Benjamin had ever seen them, even when Mom got sick last year.

Petunia giggled and rosy sparkles shone from her chestnut-colored skin. "You two are our new pair hunters. Not pear hunters, although we may do some of that in September. Our buddy finders. Dibble dabble doubles looking for two peas for a pod."

In a more serious tone, she added, "It's busy season, so we have urgent work to do!"

Elisa's eyes were now glazed with an excited curiosity.

Benjamin felt tickly flutters in his heart. He was still confused, though.

The little fairy then took in a big breath, which made her glow shimmer and shake, and told the twins the story.

Chapter 3

"When you came to Happy Valley, did you notice that it really was quite happy?" Petunia asked. "Did your heart seem to float higher than the tallest evergreen trees? Did it seem like the cherry blossoms were giggling or the flowers were smiling when you bent down to smell them?"

"The colors are definitely brighter here, and looking at the rainbows reminds me of a big hug," said Elisa "...and even the rain tastes sweet," continued Benjamin, "but I felt too silly to say that to anyone."

"Of course it does! It's not silly at all. They're candied maple drops, to be precise. My sister Silky Sugar Foot creates the rain recipes. You'll meet her later."

"If it's already such a happy place, why do you need our help?" asked Benjamin.

The twins looked at each other. "We're not magic," they said in unison.

Petunia scrunched her nose and made a bubbly sigh. "Of COURSE you're magic, silly billy pies. You have twin magic, which is a special kind of pair magic, and that's exactly what brought you here. Your mom applied for the job thanks to some of our special helpers. Because YOU have the power to help find and keep the pairings that Happy Valley needs to spread happiness."

Petunia twirled toward the twins and looked at them with her sparkling hazel eyes. "We take the business of happiness very seriously and we must spread it as far and wide as the wind blows. Luna Gloom rarely visits Happy Valley Farm, and we like to keep it that way. She is very grumpy and wears nothing but crumpled gray pajamas. Her voice turns everything around her into a storm. It's not pretty."

Elisa's eyes widened. "Who is Luna Gloom?" she asked.

"She sounds scary," Benjamin added, his face twisted with worry.

Petunia glanced up at the clear blue sky. "She used to be a fairy called Glory Moon. Her beautiful silver hair glowed just like the moon. She sprinkled a diamond powder everywhere she went, and it made the valley seem like it was coated in sparkles. Now she's dreadfully gray and spreads gloom whenever she can."

"But how did she turn into Luna Gloom?" Benjamin asked.

Petunia sighed, sending a tiny puff of stars into the air. "I'll tell you the whole story later. We have your first assignment, and it's very important to start right away." Even though this fairy was a little bossy, Benjamin was thrilled to be part of a magical little world right in their backyard. He glanced over at his sister, who looked worried.

"What do we tell mom? Do we have to keep it a secret?" Elisa asked nervously. "Oh no NO," Petunia protested. "No secrets from parents. If someone asks you to keep something a secret from your parents, the first thing you should do is run and tell your parents! Just tell your mom and she'll think you're pretending!" she added.

Petunia twirled in the air impatiently. "Well, what are we waiting for? Let's go!"

Chapter 4

The twins followed the little fairy toward the far edge of the garden. She stopped at a large painted map of Happy Valley Farm.

"This is our magical valley," she said proudly. She tapped a star at the bottom of the page and chanted, "Bright and happy, beaming too, let me see that magic in you." A colorful gleaming layer appeared upon the map.

"This is unreal!" whispered Benjamin.

"It's very real, and if you tap that very star and speak those very words, you can find the fairy map too," Petunia said in a booming voice.

"Now, let's take a little looksie here," she continued. "This map has all the details of the Happy Valley you know, but it also shows you our magical habitat within the farm." She pointed to an elegant fairy with chestnut hair near the orchard, holding a gold spoon that matched her dress. "There's my sister Silky Sugar Foot, gathering supplies for her kitchen."

Nearby, a fairy with coiled black hair was nestled in a bed of clover, sleeping peacefully. "That's Daisy Daydream," Petunia explained.

"Jolly Juniper is somewhere nearby, probably giving the bunnies a giggle. Oh! There's Innie Outie and Silly Sylvie, dancing around for their admirers near the vegetable garden." She pointed to a cheerful looking fairy with bright red hair in front of a group of squirrels. "Hilltop Holly sleeps most of the day in her den until early summer. We can also meet the lake and river fairies when the weather gets warmer. "

"Look there!" Petunia pointed to a big oyster shell under the delicate shade of the rose bush. Each half of the shell was covered in a blanket of pink petals.

"That's where Silky Sugar Foot and I sleep." She gave a little yawn. "Looking at it makes me sleepy."

Benjamin looked over the map with bright eyes. He was so excited to see the little fairies in their new backyard!

Petunia jiggled her head and rose dust fell from her long hair in a heaping pile. Energetically, she continued, "The floating gazebo is where we have our fairy gatherings. Most of our magic-making happens in the gardens and orchard," she said. Elisa asked to hear more about the magic, but the fairy rushed on.

"See here?" Petunia pointed to a spot on the map near the trail to the lake that contained a bounty of beautiful pink and purple bushes.

"Those aren't there anymore. Mom told us they got flooded out in November," said Benjamin, confused.

"They're still rebuilding the boardwalk trail," remarked Elisa.

"Exactly!" exclaimed Petunia, tiny sparks bursting from her glow.

Benjamin couldn't imagine how she had any twinkles or sparks left at the rate she was losing them.

"Happy Valley needs bushes like that for the butterflies that travel this way in September," Petunia explained. "They are special butterflies called silver-spotted skippers. If they don't have anything big and colorful to stop them, then they won't pollinate our special crop of flowers. Luna Gloom will surely settle in early for the winter if that happens. She will chase all the happiness out of our home. And if we don't have happiness to spread, who knows what'll happen in your world!" Petunia cried.

"But what about all the colorful flowers in the garden?" questioned Elisa.

Petunia Twinkletoes winked and jiggled her wings. "Excellent question. The flowers in the garden are very special and we can only grow a small amount of them. We need the butterflies to visit our garden, but we don't have enough magic flowers to attract them. We need something big that shouts at them, "Visit me!"

"Like a billboard," said Benjamin.

"Exactly," replied Petunia.

"Ok, I think understand now. Tell us how we can help you," said Benjamin.

Elisa nodded. "We don't want Luna Gloom anywhere near our new home!" She shuddered. They had enough gloom to last a lifetime when their mother got sick last year and they didn't want it chasing them over here.

"The past few years have brought more rain to the valley, and that means we need to bring in some bushes that can handle that rain," continued Petunia. "Your job is to figure out which plants would be best. We need colorful ones that can grow big."

"Like...homework?!" Benjamin asked, rather dismayed. Benjamin hated homework. This was going to be terrible.

Chapter 5

The fairy paused thoughtfully. "No.... like detective work! Remember, this is a mission. And we have magical items to help you in the library," she added. "Do you have these for homework helpers?" She opened a little bag that crossed around her tiny fairy dress. She reached in and pulled out a fairy-size pair of golden glasses, a pearl microphone, and a scepter encrusted with a rainbow of jewels. With a twirl of golden dust, the objects burst to human-size and hovered in the air.

"The glasses will help you find the information you need. Speak my name into the microphone and I will find you in a flash," Petunia explained.

"And the scepter?" asked Elisa, reaching for it. "It's warm and tingly!" she exclaimed.

"That is for the scepter to tell," Petunia replied. "It'll let you know when it's time to use it, she said mysteriously. And...they are invisible to everyone but you!"

"Whoa, cool!" exclaimed Benjamin as he gathered up the microphone and the glasses.

"Now off to work. Remember to call my name into the microphone when you need me. Ta-ta now!" A flash of dust wavered in the air and Petunia was gone.

"Wow," said Benjamin to Elisa.

"I guess it *is* pretty cool." Elisa stared back at him with nervous excitement.

"I always thought fairies were real, and this place does seem magical, but I never thought we'd actually find magic!" Benjamin said.

"I never thought we'd be in charge of such a big task," said Elisa nervously.

Benjamin ignored his sister's discomfort. "Let's get started!" he cheered.

They began their mission in the library. While Elisa loved the smell of books and paper, Benjamin preferred the sights and smells outside. He stared longingly out the window. He wished they were playing pirates by the watchtower instead. Then remembered what Petunia said about Luna Gloom and the butterflies and pulled out a few musty books from the bottom shelf, determined to help.

Finally, they found the book they were looking for. The book's title was *Plants of the Pacific Northwest.*

"Cool, the glasses are glowing!" said Benjamin, pointing to the magical items Petunia had given them earlier.

Elisa's dark curls bounced above her shoulders as she darted toward the book. "We're so close!" She said with a squeal.

Just then, their mom called them down for dinner. The twins exchanged glances. They would have to continue their mission later. Their mom, Camila Costa, was firm about nightly family dinners. They followed a fruity scent down to the dining room.

"I made cherry pie for dessert," their mother said proudly. "I can't believe how ripe these cherries are. It's so early in the season for fresh fruit. It must be magic."

"It's definitely magic," Benjamin giggled as he and Elisa exchanged knowing glances. "So where did you explore today?" their mother asked as she served them a helping of fresh vegetables from the garden. Vegetables in Happy Valley were oddly delicious. Perhaps it was because of the fairy magic.

"We went up to the watch tower, met a fairy, and then looked at her fairy home here at the farm," Benjamin said.

"You two are so silly. Where do you come up with these things?" their mom asked.

"It's our twin magic," Elisa said matter-of-factly.

Benjamin smiled in relief. Their mother thought they were joking, just like Petunia said. He was relieved that this mission did not involve lying to her because he knew it wasn't safe to keep secrets from your parents. He was glad Petunia agreed because Elisa would never lie to their mother.

Chapter 6

After dinner, they did their chores. Elisa always washed the dishes, and Benjamin dried them. When the last dish was put away, the twins raced each other back to the library. They usually played pirates on the ladder before bedtime, but tonight they were eager to get back to the book. Elisa put on the glasses. They were still glowing. She flipped through the pages, pausing from time to time. Benjamin tried to read over her shoulder, but the words were starting to scramble. The reading teacher told him that something called dyslexia made the words look like that. She said it would improve with some help and practice, but it was hard to believe. Benjamin liked to imagine that the letters were playing silly tricks on each other and he didn't know if it would be as exciting to see a page full of sleepy, still words. He used his imagination a lot last year when their mother was sick. Elisa read her books in bed and Benjamin made up silly stories that made her laugh.

"Can I see the glasses?" he asked Elisa suddenly. She zoomed them over to him like an airplane and gave them a soft landing on his nose. Benjamin smiled. He was glad his twin wasn't serious *all* the time. He looked at the page again. It looked the same as always. Except...

"Hey!" he shouted. "The glasses are talking to me." It didn't take him long to realize that the glasses were reading him the page he was on! Sometimes the teacher assigned him an audiobook for reading time and Benjamin loved to listen. The letters settled on to the page more easily when he could hear the words.

"Siberian Iris!" Elisa suddenly shouted. She was reading the book right beside him. "It can grow in flood areas and butterflies like it!"

"No, I think it says it LOOKS like a butterfly," Benjamin corrected her.

"Oh drat," said Elisa. "I thought we had it."

She paced around the room. "We need a plan. Let's make a list of all the things we are looking for. I can write and you can draw pictures." Elisa always liked to have a plan and Benjamin usually went along with it.

A short while later, they had an organized chart with pictures and a list that read:

-Ok with floods
-Colorful
-Able to grow big
-Butterflies like it

Benjamin's drawings were full of detail and color, and Elisa's writing was neat and tidy. "I think that's all we need. It'll make it easier to cross off plants that won't work," said Elisa.

"Time for bed!" called their mother from downstairs.

Benjamin looked outside. It was dark except for a scattering of twinkles which he thought must be the fairies. Suddenly his eyelids felt heavy. "I didn't know it was so late," he said.

Elisa yawned. "Let's work on this again tomorrow after school."

Sleepily, they trudged to their rooms, brushed their teeth, and went straight to bed. When their mother came up to read them bedtime stories, they were already fast asleep.

Chapter 7

The twins woke up to pale rays of sun peeking through their window, as if shyly inviting them to play in the warmth and light of a spring morning.

"I think this must be our first sunny morning since we've been here," Benjamin remarked as Elisa rubbed her eyes.

"We have a lot of work to do or else it'll be our last," Elisa warned.

Benjamin looked at her, remembering the magical events of yesterday's meeting with Petunia Twinkletoes. He would have thought it was a dream if the glasses, microphone, and scepter weren't lying on the desk across from their bunk bed.

"I still can't believe we got to meet a real fairy," Benjamin said. "I hope we meet more of them."

"I'm sure if we do a good job of finding the right butterfly plants, Petunia will introduce us to her friends and family," Elisa assured him.

After eating a breakfast of homemade bread and cherry jam with fresh eggs from the henhouse, they grabbed their backpacks and kissed their mother goodbye. Living in the city, they had always taken the bus to school. Here in Happy Valley, they were excited to be able to walk there in the fresh air, rain or shine. The road to the old schoolhouse wandered along a river path next to open fields where people brought their dogs to run around. Benjamin and Elisa loved to pet the dogs when the owners allowed it. Since today was sunny, there were more dogs than usual.

A green ball suddenly landed right in front of Elisa's feet. She bent over to pick it up and throw it back in the direction it came. A large shaggy dog came barreling over, teeth bared and growling. She froze in place, not sure what to do! Benjamin frantically looked around for a stick to ward off the mean dog.

The next moment, however, a flash of blue appeared near the dog's ear and he backed away, bowing his head as if in apology. Benjamin took the ball from Elisa and threw it in the opposite direction.

"Did you see that flash of blue? I think a fairy was here!" Benjamin exclaimed. Elisa was silent. It seemed as if she was trying to get some words out, but her mouth was frozen in place.

Benjamin realized his sister was shaken up. He shaped his hand into the form of a cup and held it close to her face. "Pretend this is a cup of hot chocolate, Vovo's special hot chocolate. Breathe in the smell of cocoa and cinnamon."

She did as she was told. "Now blow on it," he ordered. "Pretend Vovo made it too hot for you to drink." Elisa continued to follow his instructions, pretending to blow on their grandfather's famous Christmas hot chocolate. They repeated the exercise a few times until she felt better.

She looked at her brother and said gratefully, "Thank you, Benny."

"You're welcome, Lissa," he replied with a knowing smile.

"I guess twin magic doesn't always have to be about fairies and saving the world," she said thoughtfully. Benjamin nodded in agreement.

After a long morning of reading and math, the twins headed over to the library for lunch. Mr. Lee was there as usual, with a friendly smile to greet the twins.

Benjamin slung his backpack onto a nearby table and gave Mr. Lee a fist bump. "What brings you in today?" Mr. Lee asked. "I have some new Lego books if you're interested."

Before Benjamin could respond, Elisa spoke. "Actually, we are looking for a book about plants that do well in flood areas."

"Plants that butterflies would like," added Benjamin.

"That's funny." Mr. Lee rubbed his chin. "I was just looking at a book that would be perfect. Let me get it for you."

He returned with a large print book with a butterfly on the cover.

"This is the one," he announced, handing it to Elisa.

"Thank you Mr. Lee," they said.

"Any time, you two. Don't forget that it's Second Tuesday Treasure Hunt tomorrow. There'll be prizes to find before and after school," he reminded them.

"We won't miss it!" said Elisa.

"See you tomorrow!" said Benjamin.

"Our old librarian was never that fun," Elisa commented as they headed toward the lunchroom.

"Maybe it's the Happy Valley magic," suggested Benjamin.

"Nope. If it was the magic, then Mrs. Hogitha wouldn't be such a bummer," responded Elisa, referring to their grumpy second grade teacher.

Benjamin laughed. "She's probably related to Luna Gloom...."

Chapter 8

After school, the twins headed straight home to look at their new book. Out of nowhere, a gust of wind swept over the river and knocked the book out of Elisa's hands. It landed right into a muddy puddle, which happened to be the only muddy puddle on the path.

"Oh, fiddlesticks!" cried Elisa. She picked up the book carefully. It was covered in thick mud. "This is a disaster," she moaned. "We were so close to finishing the mission and now we ruined the book that we need to help us."

Benjamin hoped she wouldn't remember the library fines. That would make her even more worried. He started to say something, but the wind had gathered strength and they couldn't hear each other over the howling. It looked like a storm was coming.

A feeling of gloom settled over the twins. It didn't help that Benjamin had gotten his clothes muddy. The air was thick and wild. The twins ran against the wind all the way home. When they finally arrived, Elisa's curly brown hair was covered in leaves and twigs.

"That storm came out of nowhere," said Benjamin. He could still hear the wind howling outside and they watched as fat raindrops started to fall against the window.

"I have a funny feeling about this," said Elisa.

"Me too," said Benjamin. "The air feels funny."

"I thought it was just me," said Elisa. "Let's go see what the fairies are doing."

"Good idea," replied Benjamin.

As soon as they stepped outside, raindrops the size of crab apples pelted down on them.

"Ouch!" cried Benjamin, as they approached the map. "These raindrops are hard!"

"That's because it's starting to hail!" cried Elisa. "Let's hurry to the map!"

When they got to the map, they said the magic words together.

Bright and happy, beaming too, let me see that magic in you.

Nothing happened.

"Maybe the wind is too noisy?" asked Benjamin.

They said it again, louder this time.

BRIGHT AND HAPPY, BEAMING TOO, LET ME SEE THAT MAGIC IN YOU.

Nothing.

A sense of dread surrounded them.

"This wouldn't have happened if you didn't drop the book," he accused Elisa.

"I didn't do it on purpose!" she cried.

"Well, you should still be more careful," Benjamin said stubbornly.

"Well, YOU should be more helpful," Elisa said. "Your whining isn't helping anything."

They shuffled back toward the farmhouse, soaking wet and shivering. The rain came down even harder and thunder rumbled loudly over them, like it was shouting. Suddenly, Benjamin pointed to a frantic glow coming from the window of their room. They raced inside to find out what it was.

Chapter 9

Once they were inside, they saw that the glow was coming from the microphone. "Let's call Petunia!" Benjamin shouted.

Elisa grabbed the microphone and spoke the fairy's name again.

Suddenly, Petunia appeared in front of them. She gave a little curtsy. "At your service," she sang.

"We went to the map and said the magic words, but we couldn't see anything," Elisa said.

"How come we couldn't see you on the map?" Benjamin asked.

"We try to hide from Luna Gloom when she's here for a short visit," Petunia said with a knowing look.

"Luna Gloom is here?" Benjamin asked.

"Of course," scoffed Petunia. "Where do you think the storm came from?" She twirled her hair. "I think it's just a short visit, but if we aren't careful, she'll come back and settle in for longer next time," she added.

"You didn't tell us very much about Luna Gloom," reminded Elisa.

"How did she turn into Luna Gloom?" asked Benjamin. He didn't want to admit that he was scared, but Petunia looked at him softly with her big hazel eyes like she already understood.

"When you finish the mission, you'll understand why I haven't told you everything about her," she said softly. "What's most important to know is that she became Luna Gloom because she became afraid and started to worry. She didn't do anything about her fear except make more of it for others. She used to do things to spread happiness, even when she was feeling a little gloomy. Then she let fear and worry take over. She stopped being helpful. That's when she turned gray."

"What was she afraid of?" Elisa asked.

"We'll get to that later, I promise," said Petunia, looking in the direction of the garden. "Right now, Silky Sugar foot needs my help to sweeten her water supply, and Jolly Juniper will certainly need help comforting the bunnies. After you complete the mission, I'll tell you everything," Petunia promised. "By the way, how's the mission coming along?" she asked.

"Actually, we found a book that is going to help us!" Benjamin exclaimed.

"Excellent!" said Petunia. A thin stream of sparkles lit the air around her and she disappeared before the twins could say goodbye.

They looked at each other with worried faces.

"I'm scared we won't be able to help," Elisa admitted.

"I know," Benjamin said. "But we do have the microphone to call Petunia. We will figure out how to use the scepter and glasses to help us find the right plant. I think we can do this."

Elisa sighed, and Benjamin almost expected a puff of stars came out, like it did for Petunia.

"Let's go get the book and figure this out," Elisa said with sudden determination. The twins went back out to the hallway to get the book. The sky outside was bright blue and cloudless. If their clothes weren't soaking wet still, they might have thought they had only imagined the storm...until they went back to the book and saw it was still covered in mud.

"Oh no," groaned Elisa.

"I forgot the book was covered in mud from the puddle!" cried Benjamin. He picked up the book and tried to flip through the pages. They were soaking wet and stuck together in one big, muddy lump. "It's worse than I thought," he said gravely.

Benjamin put his hands to his face and looked at Elisa with worry in his eyes. "How are we going to help Happy Valley now?" he muttered as he slumped into a nearby chair.

Elisa sat down next to him. Her body began to slump. Suddenly, her eyes became bright and she looked at Benjamin. "Petunia told us that Glory Moon turned into Luna Gloom when she decided to worry instead of help, remember? The last thing we should do is worry." She stood up and pumped her fist in the air. "We can do this. No matter what, we will find a way to help."

Benjamin apologized to his sister. "I'm sorry I blamed you for dropping the book. I know it was just an accident."

She smiled back at him and said, "Thank you for the apology."

Just then, they heard something shaking on the desk next to their bed. It was the scepter.

Chapter 10

"The scepter!" Benjamin cried.

"I think it's trying to tell us something," said Elisa as she examined it.

Suddenly, she had an idea. "Here, put on the glasses," she instructed Benjamin.

He put on the glasses and was surprised to discover that the pages read to him through the mud! "Maybe the scepter was telling us to use the glasses," he thought aloud. "What was the name of the butterfly again?" Benjamin asked.

She looked at the tidy chart they had made.

"Silver-spotted skipper," she replied. "And we're looking for a plant that they like AND that can survive in flood areas.

"Ok, I'll look up the page for silver-spotted skippers first," he replied.

Benjamin looked through the index and the book told him the right page. After a minute, he found some information that was helpful to them. "Listen to this," he said eagerly.

Many species of butterflies and moths, including the silver-spotted skipper and the long-tailed skipper, use wisteria as a host plant. He continued. Unlike *some other types of wisteria, American Wisteria is not considered invasive in the Pacific Northwest.*

"What does that mean?" he wondered out loud.

"Remember what Mom told us about blackberry bushes?" Elisa replied. It just means they are really strong and other plants might not be able to grow well around them. Some plants are not a good fit for the environment around them." She jumped up suddenly and grabbed one of the books they were looking over yesterday. "I think

I remember something from last night!" She found the passage and slowly read it out loud.

The beautiful purple flowers of the American Wisteria will attract a lot of butterflies without harming the native ecosystem. However, it is still considered an aggressive plant and should be grown away from other flowers so that it does not overpower them. It tolerates floods and can do well in areas with heavy rainfall.

She showed him a picture of the beautiful flower climbing walls and arches in the middle of large grassy spaces.

"Good work!" Benjamin said. "It looks like it grows best when it's climbing something, like Ivy does." He paused for a moment. "But there's nothing out at the lake for it to grow on," he said with despair.

"I think if we talk to Mom or Mr. Lee, or some of the volunteers in the learning garden, we can come up with a solution," Elisa reassured him.

"I think you're right, Lissa," he said, smiling at his sister. "We don't have the perfect solution to our mission, but we just have to keep trying."

She winked at him. "We've got this, Benny."

Just then, a small swirl of blue glitter danced into the doorway.

Chapter 11

"I'm Daisy Daydream, and I think you have figured out the power of twin magic," the new fairy said with a curtsy. Her bright hair was coiled in short black curls and she had a gentle ebony face with candy apple cheeks. Her light blue dress was the color of the sky just before twilight. She brought with her a sense of peace that made the twins feel uplifted. "When you two support each other, you get places," she said in a soft, singsong voice.

Petunia zoomed right behind her, dazzling as ever.

"And when you got lost in disappointment, you almost quit," reminded Petunia in a booming voice. "The key to finishing the mission is to just keep going. You can be a part of the solution to any problem you face if you don't let worrying get in the way of using your minds."

"We didn't cry about the butterfly bushes getting lost in the floods," Daisy Daydream explained. "We took action and called for help. If we had known that we needed to try harder to explain that to Glory Moon all those years ago, then she never would have turned into Luna Gloom," Daisy said sadly.

"I didn't want to scare you earlier," Petunia said, "but the more Luna Gloom senses worry, the more she wants to be nearby to make people worry more. That's why she came for a visit, and she usually brings a storm with her. If you can help each other not to worry, then you can keep her away."

"And help others not to worry," added Daisy Daydream. "It can be really hard, but we are here to help."

Benjamin and Elisa gave each other a knowing look. They had a lot of practice helping each other to keep calm. When their mother got sick last year, they got through it together. They could do this together too.

"We are happy to help," Elisa said. "All we have left to do with the mission is get help with planting the flowers we found."

"Did you know that inviting others to help is the best way to raise hope and fight worry?" Daisy said. Her fairy glow was like a puffy cloud.

"That makes sense," said Elisa thoughtfully.

"I can't wait to see how you include others in your mission. But you better get on it, because your new mission is ready."

"What's the next mission?" Benjamin asked excitedly.

"I'll tell you all about it." Daisy said with a smile. "Better yet, let me open the dream door, and I'll show you." She twirled her fingertips and a large wooden door appeared in front of the twins. With a swirl of fairy dust, the door began to open...

Read more about the twins' adventure in The Happy Valley Twins: Daisy Daydream!

Keep in touch!

Thank you for reading!

Check out meadowhousepress.com for release dates of the next book in The Happy Valley Twins series,

and sign up for the newsletter to receive free coloring pages!

Visit our pinterest page, meadowhouselearning, to find links for creative resources in language development.